Candy Shots

Candy Shots

150 Decadent, Delicious Drinks for Your Sweet Tooth

Paul Knorr

STERLING EPICURE

An imprint of Sterling Publishing Co., Inc.

New York / London
www.sterlingpublishing.com

For Jill, and for my children Camryn, Colby, and Cooper.

Library of Congress Cataloging-in-Publication Data

Knorr, Paul.
    Candy shots : 150 decadent, delicious drinks for your sweet tooth / Paul Knorr.
            p. cm.
    Includes index.
    ISBN 978-1-4027-7125-5 (flexibound : alk. paper) 1. Bartending. 2. Cocktails. I.
Title.
    TX951.K544 2011
    641.8'74--dc22

                                        2010033276

10   9   8   7   6   5   4   3

Published by Sterling Publishing Co., Inc.
387 Park Avenue South, New York, NY 10016
© 2011 by Paul Knorr
Distributed in Canada by Sterling Publishing
C/o Canadian Manda Group, 165 Dufferin Street
Toronto, Ontario, Canada M6K 3H6
Distributed in the United Kingdom by GMC Distribution Services
Castle Place, 166 High Street, Lewes, East Sussex, England BN7 1XU
Distributed in Australia by Capricorn Link (Australia) Pty. Ltd.
P.O. Box 704, Windsor, NSW 2756, Australia

Printed in Canada
All rights reserved

Sterling ISBN 978-1-4027-7125-5

For information about custom editions, special sales, premium and
corporate purchases, please contact Sterling Special Sales
Department at 800-805-5489 or specialsales@sterlingpublishing.com.

Contents

. . . .

Introduction

One of the first drinks I learned to make and one of my favorites to serve was the Bubble Gum shot—a simple combination of Southern Comfort®, banana liqueur, grenadine, and milk. Mix equal parts of each and they make a creamy pink drink that looks, smells, and tastes just like bubble gum. Whenever there were groups of people (usually young women) who stepped up to the bar for a round of shots but were unsure just what to have, this was the drink I suggested. It not only tastes good, but it's an adult version of something everyone remembers having when they were a kid.

The drinks in this book range from the silly to the sophisticated. On the one hand there are drinks like the Girl Scout Cookie, an imitation of the classic Thin Mint® but in a shot glass. On the other hand there are drinks like a Tiramisu Martini, a sweetly elegant cocktail that when nicely garnished and presented would be right at home in any fancy restaurant. This collection tries to gather together some of the drinks that evoke classic candies and desserts, drinks that are fun to make and fun to serve. Some are appropriate as a dessert drink at a dinner party, while others are better at the bar as part of a wild night

<··· *Bubble Gum Shot, page 44*

out. What you will *not* find in this collection are the novelty shots like the Cement Mixer (vodka, Irish cream liqueur, and lime juice) or the Sweat Sock (you don't want to know). These classics have their place, but it's not here; this collection is dedicated to those shots and drinks that evoke a certain recognizable flavor.

Over the years, I've assembled a large collection of drink recipes, and many of them, especially shots, follow this format: take a candy, food, or drink that you remember from childhood and make it into an alcoholic beverage. The Tootsie Roll® (coffee liqueur and orange juice), the Jolly Rancher® (melon liqueur, peach schnapps, sweet and sour mix, and grenadine), and the Candy Apple (butterscotch schnapps and apple cider) are a few you may know. In the late eighties and early nineties, there was an explosion of new schnapps released in every flavor imaginable, from sour apple to cotton candy, and this led to an even greater variety of new drinks. Now the flavor explosion is centered on infused vodka, flavored rum, and even flavored tequila, where the taste is less cloying but still covers a wide range, from green tea to grape. By mixing these flavors with juices and sodas, it's possible to create an infinite variety of combinations. What I've gathered here are drinks whose name alone gives you a good idea of what the drink will taste like. What will a Peppermint Pattie® shot taste like? It will probably taste at least a little bit like a Peppermint Pattie®.

Drinks come in and out of fashion just like clothes and hair styles. Cocktails are becoming more and more serious, with organic vodkas, house-made sodas, and juices from locally grown produce. So-called classic cocktails are making a comeback. Drinks like the Sidecar, the Manhattan, and the Gin Fizz never really went away, but their popularity is greater than it has been since the days of war bonds and the Rat Pack. Compared to these classics, a Candy Cane shot or a shot that looks and tastes just like bubble gum can seem unsophisticated, immature, and even irresponsible. But so what? These drinks are meant to be served as shots passed around among a group of friends or teammates, accompanied by cheers and toasts. Or they are meant to be novelty drinks that double as liquid desserts.

I may be coming across as a little defensive of these silly drinks. Perhaps I am. There has been a lot of criticism recently of drinks that don't taste like alcohol, that aren't dry enough, that aren't meant for a mature palate, that aren't balanced or sophisticated.

But it was the Bubble Gum shot and others like it that inspired me to start collecting drink recipes in the late eighties. They were popular crowd-pleasers then and continue to be today, in spite of the trend toward more sophisticated "classic" cocktails. They may not be made from locally sourced all-natural ingredients. They probably have artificial flavors and almost certainly artificial colors. But they taste good, they're fun to pass around, and they make people happy. What more can you expect from a Juicy Fruit® shot or a Black Forest Cake Martini?

I think the finest compliment a bartender can receive is when a customer turns to a friend and says, "You've *got* to try this!" This is the reaction I see when I serve the drinks in this book—and it seems to happen more often with these drinks than with most others. I'm not fooling myself into thinking that I'm some kind of superstar mixologist, the Wolfgang Puck of the back bar. I suppose you could say that when I create these drinks, I'm as much a flavorist as a mixologist. With these drinks, it's all about the novelty factor, about combining unlikely ingredients to come up with a concoction that matches a specific taste memory:

"Wow! This tastes just like . . ."

Bartending Tools

BAR MATS Also known as spill stops, these mats trap spillage and keep the bar neat. They are especially handy during messy tasks such as pouring shots. Don't forget to empty the mats and wash them after each use.

BAR RAGS Always keep at least two bar rags handy to wipe up spills and keep the bar clean.

BAR SPOON A small spoon with a very long handle. It has many uses behind the bar. It can be used for stirring cocktails, of course, but you can also pour a liqueur over the back of the spoon when layering it on top of another liqueur. You can also use it to scrape the bottom of the blender.

BLENDER What bar would be complete without a blender for making fancy frozen drinks and shots? A heavy-duty, multi-speed blender is a good choice.

GARNISH TRAY Though most shots are not garnished, a nice, neat covered tray to hold your lemon slices, lime wedges, orange wheels, and cherries comes in handy when making cocktails for a crowd.

ICE SCOOP All commercial establishments require a designated scoop for use with ice, and it's wise to use an ice scoop at home as well. Ice is legally considered a food, so all the food-handling safety procedures apply. Do not use a glass to scoop the ice, or you run the risk of chipping the glass—imagine trying to find a glass chip in an ice bin! Also, keep your hands, used glassware, and any other potentially dirty objects out of contact with the ice.

JIGGER A measuring device that consists of two metal cups welded bottom to bottom. One of the cups is 1½ ounces (45 ml) and the other is 1 ounce (30 ml). Some fancier jiggers have handles.

KNIFE A good sharp knife is essential for cutting fruit for garnish. A knife can also serve as a zester and peeler. It can also be used to cut wedges and slices or to make lemon or lime twists.

LIQUOR POURS OR SPOUTS A liquor pour is used to control the flow of liquor from the bottle. This helps to prevent spilling and splashing and also controls under- or over-pouring. Most pours flow at 1 ounce per second; with a little practice and a liquor pour a bartender can accurately measure an ounce by counting.

A "measured pour" has a built-in measurement device and stops the flow after that amount.

SHAKER Also called a "cocktail shaker" or "Martini shaker," a shaker has three parts: the cup, the top, and the cap. Place ice in the cup, followed by the liquids, then press the top and the cap on tightly and shake (away from the customer!). To serve, remove the cap and use the top as a strainer.

BOSTON SHAKER This is a less elegant, but easier, cheaper, and more reliable alternative to the Martini shaker. it consists of a metal cup and a pint glass. Place ice and liquids in the cup, press the glass tightly over the cup to form a seal, shake, and serve. Since a Boston shaker does not have a strainer built in, you will need a separate strainer to hold back the ice as you pour.

STRAINER A strainer fits over the top of a Boston shaker or any other glass and is used to strain the ice from a drink after it's been stirred or shaken.

Glassware

COCKTAIL GLASS A stemmed, inverted-triangle-shaped glass. The size varies widely, from 4 to 12 ounces.

COLLINS GLASS A tall, narrow tumbler that usually holds around 14 ounces.

COUPETTE GLASS Also called a Margarita glass, this stemmed glass is flat and has a wide rim. The most common size is 12 ounces.

SHOT GLASS A small 1½-ounce glass.

Bartending Techniques

All the shot and shooter recipes in this book give measurements in equal "parts," as in 1 part this and 2 parts that. This serves several purposes. First, it makes the recipes work even if you're metrically challenged, as there's no need to convert between ounces and centiliters. Listing the proportions also will allow for different-sized glassware, and for making drinks in quantities greater than one—after all, if you're making Creamsicle® shots, you're probably among friends, so it's only polite to make more than one at a time. Most of the cocktail and Martini recipes here use ounce and volume measurements, since the proportions in such drinks can tend to be a bit more complex than those in shots.

SHAKE WITH ICE AND STRAIN. Fill the cup or a cocktail or Boston shaker with ice, add the ingredients, and cover it with the lid. Shake it briskly until the outside begins to frost, then take the top lid off (for a cocktail shaker) or remove the pint glass and place the strainer over the cup (for a Boston shaker) and strain the drink into the glass, leaving the ice behind in the shaker.

LAYER IN THE GLASS. Pour each of the ingredients into the shot glass, keeping each ingredient on its own distinct layer. To achieve the layering effect, place a bar spoon upside down against the inner rim of the glass, just above the first ingredient. Gently pour the next ingredient over the back of the spoon to prevent the liquor from entering the glass too quickly and therefore mixing with the previous ingredient. For these types of drinks, the order is important; for best results pour in the order listed, heavier ingredients first.

BUILD OVER ICE. Fill the glass with ice and add the ingredients, allowing them to mix naturally.

BUILD OVER ICE AND STIR. Fill the glass with ice, add the ingredients, and stir the drink with a stir stick or bar spoon.

BUILD IN THE GLASS WITH NO ICE. Add the ingredients to the glass without ice. This is typically called for when the ingredients are already cold and should not be diluted with ice.

COMBINE ALL THE INGREDIENTS IN A BLENDER WITH ICE. BLEND UNTIL SMOOTH. Add ice to the blender and then add all the ingredients. Blend everything until smooth.

Glossary of Ingredients

AMARETTO An Italian liqueur made from apricot kernels and seeds combined with almond extract steeped in brandy and sweetened with sugar syrup. *Amaretto* is Italian for "a little bitter."

ANISETTE An Italian anise-flavored liqueur mainly consumed in France and Spain. It is sweeter than most anise-flavored liqueurs (such as pastis or Pernod®), and also has a lower alcohol content (typically 25 percent by volume, versus 40 percent in most others).

APPLEJACK An alcoholic beverage, produced from apples, that originated during the American colonial period. It is made by concentrating hard cider, either by the traditional method of freeze distillation or by true evaporative distillation. The term "applejack" is derived from "jacking," an expression referring to freeze distillation.

BITTERS Bitter-tasting herbal flavorings. Originally marketed as patent medicines, the few remaining varieties (such as Angostura®, curaçao, orange, and Peychaud's® bitters) are principally used as a flavoring in food recipes or in cocktails.

BLACKCURRANT CORDIAL A black currant-infused liqueur.

MOZART® BLACK CHOCOLATE LIQUEUR A dark chocolate– and vanilla-flavored liqueur.

BOURBON An American form of whiskey made from at least 51 percent corn, with the remainder being wheat or rye and malted barley. It is distilled to no more than 160 proof (80 percent alcohol by volume) and aged in new charred white-oak barrels for at least two years. It must be put into the barrels at no more than 125 U.S. proof.

BRANDY A liquor made from distilled wine (fermented grape juice) or other fermented fruit juice.

CALVADOS An apple brandy from the French region of Lower Normandy.

CHARTREUSE® A famous French liqueur produced by the Carthusian monks, from a formula created in 1605 that contains 130 herbs and spices. Green Chartreuse® is 55 percent alcohol by volume and naturally green in color. The color chartreuse is named after this liqueur.

COINTREAU® A fine, colorless, orange-flavored liqueur made from the dried skins of oranges grown on the island of Curaçao in the Dutch West Indes. The generic term for this type of liqueur is Curaçao; if it is redistilled and clarified, it is called triple sec.

CRÈME LIQUEURS Crème liqueurs are very sweet, with a single flavor that dominates.

CRÈME DE ALMOND Almond-flavored sweet liqueur.

CRÈME DE BANANA Banana-flavored sweet liqueur.

CRÈME DE CACAO (DARK) Chocolate-flavored sweet liqueur that is dark brown in color.

CRÈME DE CACAO (WHITE) Colorless chocolate-flavored sweet liqueur.

CRÈME DE COCONUT Coconut-flavored sweet liqueur.

CRÈME DE MENTHE (GREEN) Mint-flavored sweet liqueur that is green in color.

CRÈME DE MENTHE (WHITE) Colorless mint-flavored sweet liqueur.

CRÈME DE NOYAUX Sweet liqueur made from fruit pits; has a bitter almond flavor.

DR. MCGILLICUDDY'S INTENSE MENTHOLMINT SCHNAPPS® A schnapps made by the Sazerac company that is strongly flavored with menthol and mint.

FRANGELICO® An Italian brand of hazelnut-flavored liqueur packaged in a distinctive monk-shaped bottle.

GIN Gin begins as a neutral spirit. It is then redistilled with or filtered through juniper berries and botanicals such as coriander seeds, cassia bark, orange peels, fennel seeds, anise, caraway, angelica root, licorice, lemon peel, almonds, cinnamon bark, bergamot, and cocoa; it is this secondary process that imparts to each gin its particular taste.

GODIVA® LIQUEUR A neutral spirit–based liqueur flavored with Godiva® brand Belgian chocolate and other flavors. There are currently four types: milk chocolate, original chocolate, white chocolate, and mocha.

GOLDSCHLÄGER® A cinnamon-flavored liqueur produced in Switzerland that includes flakes of real gold in the bottle.

GRAND MARNIER® A French brand of orange-flavored liqueur (triple sec) with a brandy base.

GRENADINE A sweet syrup made from pomegranate juice, containing little or no alcohol.

HOT DAMN!® CINNAMON SCHNAPPS A brand of cinnamon-flavored liqueur with a strong cinnamon flavor and a red color.

IRISH CREAM LIQUEUR A mocha-flavored whiskey and double-cream liqueur, combining Irish whiskey, cream, coffee, chocolate, and other flavors.

JACK DANIEL'S® A whiskey made in Tennessee that is perhaps the most famous whiskey made in America. The Jack Daniel's distillery in Lynchburg, Tennessee, dates from 1875 and is the oldest registered distillery in the United States. Jack Daniel's® is made according to the sour-mash process, and by the "Lincoln County Process" of filtration through sugar maple charcoal before being aged in charred American oak casks.

JÄGERMEISTER® A complex, aromatic liqueur containing 56 herbs, roots, and fruits that has been popular in Germany since its introduction in 1935. In Germany it is frequently consumed warm as an aperitif or after-dinner drink. In the United States it is widely popular as a chilled shooter.

KIRSCHWASSER A clear brandy made from double distillation of the fermented juice of black cherries.

LICOR 43® (CUARENTA Y TRES) A yellow-colored liqueur from Spain made from 43 ingredients including fruit juices, vanilla, and other aromatic herbs and spices.

MARASCHINO LIQUEUR A very sweet white cherry liqueur made from the marasca cherry of Dalmatia, Yugoslavia.

MELON LIQUEUR A pale green liqueur that tastes of fresh muskmelon or cantaloupe. The most famous brand, Midori®, is Japanese in origin and is produced by the Suntory Company in Mexico, France, and Japan.

OUZO An anise-flavored liqueur from Greece, usually served on the rocks. Ouzo can be used as a substitute for absinthe in many cases.

PASTIS A semisweet anise-flavored liqueur produced to be a substitute for absinthe.

PERNOD® A brand of pastis produced by the Pernod-Ricard company.

REDRUM® A brand of 70-proof tropical fruit–flavored rum.

RUM A liquor made from fermented and distilled sugarcane juice or molasses. Rum has a wide range of flavors, from light and dry like a vodka to very dark and complex like a cognac.

LIGHT RUM Clear in color and dry in flavor.

SPICED RUM The original flavored rum. Spiced rum consists of an amber rum with vanilla and cinnamon flavors added.

Rumple Minze® A 100-proof peppermint schnapps produced in Germany.

Sambuca An Italian liqueur flavored with anise and elderberry, produced in both clear ("white sambuca") and dark blue or purple ("black sambuca") versions.

Schnapps A liqueur distilled from grains, roots, or fruits. Real schnapps has no sugar or flavoring added, as the flavor should originate from the base material. Many syrupy sweet fruit liqueurs are called schnapps, but they are not true schnapps because they have both sugar and flavorings added.

Simple Syrup A combination of equal parts sugar and boiling water that, once cool, is used as a sweetener in many mixed drinks.

Sloe Gin A liqueur flavored with sloe berries and blackthorn fruit. It traditionally was made with a gin base with sugar added, but most modern versions use a neutral spirit base and add flavorings later.

Sour Mix A syrup made from a blend of sugar and lemon juice. A simple recipe is to mix equal parts simple syrup and lemon juice.

Southern Comfort® A liqueur with a neutral spirit base and peach and almond flavors.

Sweetened Lime Juice As the name would imply, lime juice with sugar added.

Tabasco® Sauce A brand of hot pepper sauce made from a blend of Tabasco peppers, vinegar, and salt, aged in wood casks.

Tequila A type of mescal that is made only from the blue agave plant in the region surrounding Tequila, a town in the Mexican state of Jalisco. Tequila is made in many different styles, with the difference between them dependent on how long the distillate has been aged before being bottled.

Tia Maria® A brand of coffee-flavored liqueur from Jamaica. Tia Maria® is Jamaican rum–based and flavored with spices.

Triple Sec A highly popular flavoring agent in many drinks, triple sec is the best known form of curaçao, a liqueur made from the skins of the curaçao orange.

Vermouth A fortified wine flavored with aromatic herbs and spices. There are three common varieties of vermouth.

- **Dry Vermouth** Clear or pale yellow in color and very dry in flavor.
- **Sweet Vermouth** Red in color and sweeter than dry vermouth.

- **White Vermouth** Clear or pale yellow in color, but sweeter than dry vermouth.

VODKA A neutral spirit that can be distilled from almost anything that will ferment (grain, potatoes, grapes, corn, and beets). It is distilled multiple times, filtered to remove impurities, then diluted with water to bring the alcohol content down before it is bottled. Vodka is sold in a wide variety of flavors, from bison grass to watermelon.

WHISKEY (OR WHISKY) A beverage distilled from fermented grain and aged in oak casks. The location, grain, type of oak, and length of the aging all affect the flavor of the whiskey. Whiskey is spelled with an "e" in Ireland and the United States and without the "e" everywhere else. There are four major regions where whiskey is produced: Ireland, Scotland, Canada, and the United States. Each has a different style that imparts a distinctive flavor.

The Drinks

. . . .

A Joy of Almond

2 parts Coffee Liqueur
1 part Amaretto
1 part Crème de Noyaux

Shake with ice and strain.

Cocktail Glass

A Sundae on Sunday

1 part Light Rum
1 part Amaretto
1 part Coconut Cream
splash Cherry Syrup
splash Milk

Combine all the ingredients in a blender with ice. Blend until smooth. Note: Because this recipe includes many ingredients, it's easier to make in volume, about 6 shots.

Coupette Glass

Acid Cookie

1 part Irish Cream Liqueur
1 part Butterscotch Schnapps
1 part Hot Damn!® Cinnamon Schnapps
splash 151-Proof Rum

Shake with ice and strain.

Shot Glass

Adult Kool-Aid®

1 oz. Amaretto
1 oz. Grenadine
1 oz. Melon Liqueur
2 oz. Pineapple Juice
1½ oz. Sour Mix

Build over ice and stir. Note: Because this recipe includes many ingredients, it's easier to make in volume, about 6 shots.

Collins Glass

After-Dinner Mint

1½ oz. Southern Comfort®
½ oz. Vodka
½ oz. Crème de Menthe (White)
fill with Hot Cocoa

Combine all the ingredients in an Irish Coffee mug.
If desired, garnish with whipped cream and an
Andes® mint.

Irish Coffee Mug

After Eight® Thin Mint

1 part Crème de Cacao (White)
1 part Crème de Menthe (Green)
1 part Irish Cream Liqueur

Combine in the glass.

Shot Glass

Airhead

1 part Peach Schnapps
1 part Cranberry Juice Cocktail

Shake with ice and strain.

Shot Glass

Almond Cookie

1 part Amaretto
1 part Butterscotch Schnapps

Shake with ice and strain.

Shot Glass

Almond Joy® Shot

1 part Amaretto
1 part Irish Cream Liqueur
1 part Swiss Chocolate Almond Liqueur

Combine in the glass.

Shot Glass

Almond Joy®
Shot in the Dark

2 parts Coconut-Flavored Rum
1 part Mozart® Black Chocolate Liqueur
1 part Amaretto

Shake with ice and strain.

Shot Glass

Almond Joy® Cocktail

½ oz. Amaretto
½ oz. Crème de Cacao (White)
2 oz. Light Cream

Shake with ice and strain.

Cocktail Glass

Almond Joy® Cocktail 2

½ oz. Coconut-Flavored Rum
1 oz. Amaretto
1 oz. Crème de Cacao (White)
2 oz. Cream

Shake with ice and strain.

Cocktail Glass

Almond Joy® Martini

2 parts Coconut-Flavored Rum
1 part Mozart® Black Chocolate Liqueur
splash Frangelico®

Shake with ice and strain.

Cocktail Glass

Amaretto Lemon Drop

1 oz. Vodka
1 oz. Amaretto
fill with Lemonade

Build over ice and stir.

Collins Glass

Andes® Candy

1 part Frangelico®
1 part Rumple Minze®

Shake with ice and strain.

Shot Glass

Apple Pie
à la Mode

1 oz. Spiced Rum
½ oz. Sour Apple Schnapps
2 oz. Apple Juice
1 oz. Crème de Coconut
1 oz. Heavy Cream
dash Cinnamon

*Combine all the ingredients in a blender
with ice. Blend until smooth.*

Coupette Glass

Apple Sweet Tart

1 part Vodka
1 part Sour Apple Schnapps
1 part Cherry Juice
1 part Wild Berry Schnapps
1 part Lemonade

Shake with ice and strain. Note: It's easier to make this recipe in volume, about 6 shots.

Shot Glass

Apple Pie Cocktail

1 oz. Light Rum
½ oz. Sweet Vermouth
splash Applejack
splash Lemon Juice
splash Grenadine

Shake with ice and strain.

Cocktail Glass

32

Apple Pie Shooter

4 parts Sour Apple Schnapps
1 part Cinnamon Schnapps

Shake with ice and strain.

Shot Glass

Apple Pie with a Crust

1 part Coconut-Flavored Rum
3 parts Apple Juice
dash Cinnamon Schnapps

Shake with ice and strain.

Shot Glass

Aquarium Jell-O®

4 packages Blue Raspberry Jell-O®
2 cups Vodka
2 cups Cold Water
4 cups Boiling Water
1 cup Jelly Beans
5 pieces Gummy Fish

Use a new and well-cleaned goldfish bowl. Mix gelatin in a separate bowl according to package directions, substituting vodka for half the cold water. Place the jelly beans in the bowl. When gelatin is cool but not yet setting up, pour it slowly into the bowl, being careful not to disturb the jelly beans or their color will run. Cool until half-set, then add gummy fish, placing them using strands of spaghetti to manuever them into the gelatin. Refrigerate until serving time.

Fish Bowl

Astropop

1 part Grenadine
1 part Amaretto
1 part Rumple Minze®

Layer in the glass.

Shot Glass

Banana Split Cocktail

½ oz. Vodka
1½ oz. Crème de Banana
1 oz. Crème de Cacao (White)
1 oz. Light Cream

Shake with ice and strain.

Cocktail Glass

Banana Split Shooter

1 part Chocolate Liqueur
1 part Strawberry Liqueur
1 part Banana Liqueur

Combine in the glass.

Shot Glass

Replace Chocolate Liqueur with Coffee Liqueur for another variation!

Big Red

1 part Irish Cream Liqueur
1 part Goldschläger®

Shake with ice and strain.

Shot Glass

Big Red 2

1 part Goldschläger®
splash Cranberry Juice Cocktail

Shake with ice and strain.

Shot Glass

Bit-O-Honey®

1 part Butterscotch Schnapps
1 part Irish Cream Liqueur

Combine in the glass.

Shot Glass

Bit-O-Honey® 2

1 part Apple Brandy
1 part Frangelico®

Combine in the glass.

Shot Glass

Black Forest Cake

1 part Kirschwasser
1 part Coffee Liqueur
1 part Irish Cream Liqueur

Shake with ice and strain.

Shot Glass

Black Forest Cake Martini

1½ oz. Vodka
1 oz. Crème de Cacao (White)
splash Raspberry Liqueur

Shake with ice and strain.

Cocktail Glass

Bubble Gum

1 part Southern Comfort®
1 part Crème de Banana
1 part Grenadine
1 part Milk

Shake with ice and strain.

Shot Glass

Bubble Gum 2

1 part Melon Liqueur
1 part Vodka
1 part Crème de Banana
1 part Orange Juice

Shake with ice and strain.

Shot Glass

Bubble Gum 3

1 part Crème de Banana
1 part Melon Liqueur
1 part Vodka
1 part Grenadine
1 part Orange Juice
1 part Sour Mix

Shake with ice and strain. Note: Because this recipe includes many ingredients, it's easier to make in volume, about 6 shots.

Shot Glass

Bubble Gum 4

2 parts Southern Comfort®
2 parts Blackberry Brandy
1 part Grenadine
1 part Light Cream

Shake with ice and strain.

Shot Glass

Blackberry Sourball

1 part Vodka
1 part Blackberry Liqueur
splash Lemonade
splash Orange Juice

Shake with ice and strain.

Shot Glass

Black Licorice

1 part Coffee Liqueur
1 part Sambuca

Shake with ice and strain.

Shot Glass

Buttered Toffee

½ oz. Coffee Liqueur
½ oz. Irish Cream Liqueur
½ oz. Amaretto
2 oz. Half and Half

Shake with ice and strain.

Cocktail Glass

Candy Apple

1 part Butterscotch Schnapps
1 part Apple Cider

Shake with ice and strain.

Shot Glass

Candy Apple 2

2 parts Amaretto
1 part Butterscotch Schnapps
2 parts Apple Juice

Shake with ice and strain.

Shot Glass

Candy Apple Martini

1½ oz. Peach Schnapps
1½ oz. Calvados
½ oz. Cranberry Juice Cocktail

Shake with ice and strain.

Cocktail Glass

Candy Bar

1 oz. Coffee Liqueur
1 oz. Light Cream
½ oz. Crème de Cacao (White)
½ oz. Frangelico®

Shake with ice and strain.

Cocktail Glass

Candy Cane

1 part Grenadine
1 part Crème de Menthe (White)
1 part Peppermint Schnapps

Layer in the glass.

Shot Glass

Candy Cane 2

1 part Crème de Cacao (White)
1 part Vodka
1 part Grenadine

Layer in the glass.

Shot Glass

Candy Corn

1 part Licor 43®
1 part Blue Curaçao
1 part Light Cream

Combine in the glass.

Shot Glass

Candy from Strangers

1½ oz. Vodka
½ oz. Triple Sec
½ oz. Amaretto
½ oz. Dry Vermouth

Shake with ice and strain.

Cocktail Glass

Caramel

1 part Coffee Liqueur
1 part Pineapple Juice

Shake with ice and strain.

Shot Glass

Caramel Apple

1 part Sour Apple Schnapps
1 part Butterscotch Schnapps

Shake with ice and strain.

Shot Glass

Caramel Apple Martini

2 parts Butterscotch Schnapps
2 parts Sour Apple Schnapps
1 part Vodka

Shake with ice and strain.

Cocktail Glass

Cheesecake

1 part Cranberry Juice Cocktail
1 part Vanilla Liqueur

Shake with ice and strain.

Shot Glass

Cheesecake Martini

1 oz. Vanilla-Flavored Vodka
½ oz. Triple Sec
½ oz. Sour Mix
1 oz. Light Cream
dash Crème de Cacao (White)

*Shake with ice and strain. Note: Because this recipe
includes many ingredients, it's easier to make in
volume, about 6 shots.*

Cocktail Glass

Cherry Life Saver®

1 part Southern Comfort®
1 part Amaretto
2 parts Sour Mix
splash Grenadine

Shake with ice and strain.

Shot Glass

Cherry Lollipop

1 part Vodka
1 part Lemonade
1 part Cherry Juice

Shake with ice and strain.

Shot Glass

Chocolate Chip Shooter

1 part Amaretto
1 part Crème de Cacao (White)
1 part Irish Cream Liqueur

Shake with ice and strain.

Shot Glass

Chocolate-Covered Almond

1 part Amaretto
1 part Crème de Cacao (Dark)
1 part Light Cream

Shake with ice and strain.

Shot Glass

Chocolate-Covered Cherry

1 part Coffee Liqueur
1 part Amaretto
1 part Crème de Cacao (White)
splash Grenadine

Shake with ice and strain.

Shot Glass

Chocolate-Covered Banana

1 part Vodka
1 part Crème de Cacao (Dark)
1 part Crème de Banana
1 part Light Cream

Shake with ice and strain.

Shot Glass

Chocolate-Dipped Strawberry

1 part Godiva® Liqueur
1 part Tequila Rose®

Shake with ice and strain.

Shot Glass

Chocolate-Covered Raspberry

1 part Crème de Cacao (White)
1 part Raspberry Liqueur

Shake with ice and strain.

Shot Glass

Chocolate Martini

2 parts Vodka
1 part Crème de Cacao (White)

Shake with ice and strain.

Cocktail Glass

Chocolate Martini 2

3 parts Vanilla-Flavored Vodka
2 parts Godiva® Liqueur

Shake with ice and strain.

Cocktail Glass

Chocolate Pudding

1 part Crème de Cacao (White)
1 part Hazelnut Liqueur
1 part Light Cream

Shake with ice and strain.

Cocktail Glass

Chocolate Sundae

1 part Irish Cream Liqueur
1 part Crème de Cacao (White)
1 part Coffee Liqueur
top with Whipped Cream

Combine in the glass.

Shot Glass

Cinnamon Apple Pie

3 parts Sour Apple Schnapps
1 part Cinnamon Schnapps

Shake with ice and strain.

Shot Glass

Cinnamon Roll

1 part Irish Cream Liqueur
1 part Cinnamon Schnapps

Shake with ice and strain.

Shot Glass

Creamsicle®

1 part Vanilla-Flavored Vodka
1 part Milk
1 part Orange Juice

Shake with ice and strain.

Shot Glass

Creamsicle® Martini

1½ oz. Vanilla Liqueur
½ oz. Grand Marnier®
splash Orange Juice

Shake with ice and strain.

Cocktail Glass

Dark Chocolate Martini

. . . .

2 oz. Vodka
1 oz. Black Mozart® Chocolate Liqueur
splash Heavy Cream

Shake with ice and strain.

Cocktail Glass

Dirty Girl Scout Cookie

. . . .

1 part Coffee Liqueur
1 part Irish Cream Liqueur
1 part Crème de Menthe (White)

Shake with ice and strain.

Shot Glass

Doublemint

1 part Dr. McGillicuddy's Intense Mentholmint
    Schnapps®
1 part Coffee Liqueur
splash Crème de Menthe (Green)

Shake with ice and strain.

Shot Glass

Doublemint Delight

1 part Dr. McGillicuddy's Intense Mentholmint
    Schnapps®
1 part Coffee Liqueur
2 parts Light Cream

Shake with ice and strain.

Shot Glass

Froot Loops®

1½ oz. Sour Apple Schnapps
2 oz. Orange Juice

Shake with ice and strain.

Cocktail Glass

Froot Loops® 2

1 part Amaretto
1 part Blue Curaçao
1 part Grenadine
1 part Milk

Shake with ice and strain.

Shot Glass

Fruity Pebbles®

1 part Vodka
1 part Blue Curaçao
1 part Milk
dash Grenadine

Shake with ice and strain.

Shot Glass

Fruity Pebbles® 2

1 part Blue Curaçao
1 part Raspberry Liqueur
2 parts Milk

Shake with ice and strain.

Shot Glass

Gingerbread

1 part Irish Cream Liqueur
1 part Goldschläger®
1 part Butterscotch Schnapps

Combine in the glass.

Shot Glass

Gingerbread Man

1 part Goldschläger®
1 part Irish Cream Liqueur
1 part Butterscotch Schnapps
1 part Vodka

Shake with ice and strain.

Shot Glass

Gingersnap

1 part Coffee Liqueur
1 part Irish Cream Liqueur
1 part Frangelico®
1 part Jägermeister®
1 part Cola

*Shake with ice and strain. Note: Because this recipe
includes many ingredients, it's easier to make in
volume, about 6 shots.*

Shot Glass

Girl Scout Cookie

2 parts Coffee Liqueur
1 part Peppermint Schnapps
2 parts Light Cream

Shake with ice and strain.

Shot Glass

Good & Plenty®

1 part Bailey's Irish Cream®
1 part Sambuca
1 splash Soda

Build over ice or combine all ingredients in a blender with ice until smooth.

Highball Glass

Good & Plenty® 2

1 oz. Sambuca
Dr. Pepper®

Build over ice.

Collins Glass

Grape Kool-Aid®

1 part Blue Curaçao
1 part Southern Comfort®
1 part Raspberry Liqueur
1 part Pineapple Juice
1 part Sour Mix
2 parts Cranberry Juice Cocktail

Shake with ice and strain. Note: Because this recipe includes many ingredients, it's easier to make in volume, about 6 shots.

Shot Glass

Gumball

2 parts Blue Curaçao
1 part Vodka
1 part Crème de Banana
top with Ginger Ale

Shake with ice and strain. Top with a splash of ginger ale.

Shot Glass

Gumball Hummer

1 part Raspberry Liqueur
1 part Banana Liqueur
1 part Grapefruit Juice

Shake with ice and strain.

Shot Glass

Gumball Martini

2 oz. Gin
1 oz. Vodka
½ oz. Southern Comfort®
¼ oz. Dry Vermouth

Shake with ice and strain.

Cocktail Glass

Gumball Shooter

1 part Blue Curaçao
1 part Crème de Banana
1 part Sambuca

Shake with ice and strain.

Shot Glass

Gummy Bear Martini

2 oz. Gin
1 oz. RedRum®
splash Pink Lemonade

Shake with ice and strain. Garnish with a cherry.

Cocktail Glass

Gummy Bear Shot

1 part Southern Comfort®
1 part Amaretto
1 part Grenadine
1 part Melon Liqueur
2 parts Orange Juice
2 parts Pineapple Juice

Shake with ice and strain. Note: It's easier to make this recipe in volume, about 6 shots.

Shot Glass

Hawaiian Punch

1 part Southern Comfort®
1 part Sloe Gin
1 part Orange Juice
1 part Amaretto

Shake with ice and strain.

Shot Glass

Hawaiian Punch from Hell

1 part Vodka
1 part Southern Comfort®
1 part Amaretto
splash Orange Juice
splash Lemon-Lime Soda
splash Grenadine

Shake with ice and strain. Note: Because this recipe includes many ingredients, it's easier to make in volume, about 6 shots.

Shot Glass

Hot Apple Pie

1 part Cinnamon Schnapps
1 part Sour Apple Schnapps

Shake with ice and strain.

Shot Glass

Ice Cream Shot

1 part Vanilla Liqueur
1 part Irish Cream Liqueur

Shake with ice and strain.

Shot Glass

Jelly Belly®

1 part Blackberry Liqueur
1 part Peppermint Liqueur
1 part Bourbon

Shake with ice and strain.

Shot Glass

Jelly Bean

1 part Blackberry Brandy
1 part Peppermint Schnapps

Shake with ice and strain.

Shot Glass

Jelly Bean 2

1 part Coffee Liqueur
1 part Anisette
1 part 151-Proof Rum

Shake with ice and strain.

Shot Glass

Jolly Rancher®

2 parts Melon Liqueur
1 part Peach Schnapps
1 part Sour Mix
splash Grenadine

Shake with ice and strain.

Shot Glass

Jolly Rancher® 2

1 part Sour Apple Schnapps
1 part Peach Schnapps
1 part Cranberry Juice Cocktail

Shake with ice and strain.

Shot Glass

Jolly Rancher® 3

1 part Vodka
1 part Peach Schnapps
1 part Cranberry Juice Cocktail
1 part Pineapple Juice

Shake with ice and strain.

Shot Glass

Juicy Fruit®

2 parts Raspberry Liqueur
1 part Triple Sec
1 part Melon Liqueur

Shake with ice and strain.

Shot Glass

Juicy Fruit® Remix

1 part Vodka
1 part Crème de Banana
1 part Peach Schnapps
1 part Cranberry Juice Cocktail
1 part Lemonade
1 part Orange Juice

Shake with ice and strain. Note: Because this recipe includes many ingredients, it's easier to make in volume, about 6 shots.

Shot Glass

Junior Mint®

1 part Peppermint Schnapps
1 part Crème de Cacao (Dark)

Shake with ice and strain.

Shot Glass

Junior Mint® 2

1 part Irish Cream Liqueur
1 part Godiva® Liqueur
1 part Rumple Minze®

Shake with ice and strain.

Shot Glass

Key Lime Pie

. . . .

2 parts Licor 43®
2 parts Half and Half
1 part Lime Juice

Shake with ice and strain.

Shot Glass

Key Lime Shooter

. . . .

2 parts Licor 43®
1 part Light Rum
1 part Sour Mix
splash Sweetened Lime Juice
splash Half and Half

Shake with ice and strain. Note: Because this recipe includes many ingredients, it's easier to make in volume, about 6 shots.

Shot Glass

100

Kool-Aid®

....

1 part Vodka
1 part Amaretto
1 part Melon Liqueur
1 part Raspberry Liqueur

Shake with ice and strain.

Shot Glass

Kool-Aid® (Southern Style)

....

1 part Amaretto
1 part Southern Comfort®
1 part Cranberry Juice Cocktail
splash Grenadine

Shake with ice and strain.

Shot Glass

Lemon Drop Cocktail

2 oz. Vodka
1 oz. Triple Sec
splash Lemon Juice

Shake with ice and strain.

Cocktail Glass

Lemon Drop Shooter

1 oz. Vodka
1 wedge Lemon
1 Sugar Packet or 1 tsp. sugar

Shake the vodka with ice and strain. Pour the sugar packet onto the lemon wedge. Drink the shot and bite down on the lemon wedge.

Shot Glass

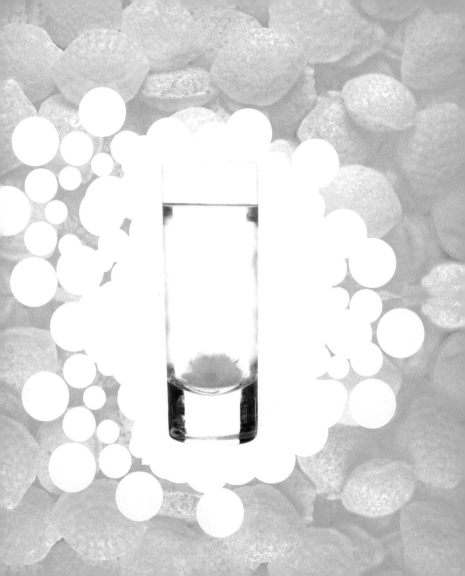

Lemon Meringue

1 part Vodka
1 part Lemon Juice
dab of Whipped Cream

Shake with ice and strain.
Top with whipped cream.

Shot Glass

Licorice Stick

1 oz. Black Sambuca
1 oz. Vodka
½ oz. Crème de Cacao (White)

Shake with ice and strain.

Cocktail Glass

Licorice Twist

1 part Blackcurrant Cordial
1 part Pernod®
2 parts Lemonade

Shake with ice and strain.

Cocktail Glass

Life Saver®

1 oz. Light Rum
1 oz. Pineapple Juice
¼ oz. Lime Juice
dash Blue Curaçao
dash Triple Sec
dash Simple Syrup

Shake with ice and strain.

Cocktail Glass

Liquid Snickers®

2 parts Crème de Cacao (Dark)
1 part Irish Cream Liqueur
1 part Frangelico®
1 part Light Cream

Shake with ice and strain.

Shot Glass

Lollipop Cocktail

1½ oz. Cointreau®
1 oz. Kirschwasser
splash Green Chartreuse®
splash Cherry Liqueur

Shake with ice and strain.

Cocktail Glass

Melon Ball Shooter

2 parts Melon Liqueur
1 part Vodka
1 part Orange Juice

Shake with ice and strain.

Shot Glass

Mint Chocolate Chip

1 part Crème de Menthe (Green)
1 part Crème de Cacao (White)

Shake with ice and strain.

Shot Glass

Peanut Butter and Jelly

....

1 part Frangelico®
1 part Raspberry Liqueur

Shake with ice and strain.

Shot Glass

Peanut Butter Chocolate Chip Cookie

....

1 part Frangelico®
1 part Tia Maria®
1 part Coffee Liqueur

Shake with ice and strain.

Shot Glass

Peanut Butter Cup

½ oz. Vodka
½ oz. Frangelico®
½ oz. Crème de Cacao (White)
2 oz. Light Cream

Shake with ice and strain.

Cocktail Glass

Peppermint Pattie®

1 part Coffee Liqueur
1 part Peppermint Schnapps
1 part Light Cream

Shake with ice and strain.

Shot Glass

Peppermint Pattie® 2

1 part Rumple Minze®
1 part Crème de Cacao (Dark)

Shake with ice and strain.

Shot Glass

Pixy Stix® Cocktail

1½ oz. Light Rum
½ oz. Apricot Brandy
2 tsp. Lime Juice
2 tsp. Lemon Juice
1 tsp. Sugar

Shake with ice and strain.

Cocktail Glass

Pixy Stix®

1 part Vodka
1 part Apricot Brandy
1 part Blue Curaçao
1 part Grape Schnapps
1 part Lemonade

Shake with ice and strain. Note: Because this recipe includes many ingredients, it's easier to make in volume, about 6 shots.

Shot Glass

Pumpkin Pie

2 parts Coffee Liqueur
1 part Irish Cream Liqueur
1 part Goldschläger®

Shake with ice and strain.

Shot Glass

Popsicle®

1 part Amaretto
1 part Orange Juice
1 part Light Cream

Shake with ice and strain.

Shot Glass

Raspberry Brownie

1 part Coffee Liqueur
1 part Raspberry Liqueur
1 part Light Cream

Combine in the glass.

Shot Glass

Red Hots®

1 part Cinnamon Schnapps
dash Tabasco® Sauce

Build in the glass with no ice.

Shot Glass

Skittles®

1 part Vodka
1 part Southern Comfort®
1 part Melon Liqueur
1 part Pineapple Juice
1 part Sour Mix

Shake with ice and strain. Note: Because this recipe includes many ingredients, it's easier to make in volume, about 6 shots.

Shot Glass

Smarties®

1 part Grape-Flavored Schnapps
1 part Melon Liqueur

Shake with ice and strain.

Shot Glass

Snickers®

1 part Crème de Cacao (Dark)
1 part Frangelico®

Shake with ice and strain.

Shot Glass

Sno-Caps®

1 part Irish Cream Liqueur
1 part Tequila

Combine in the glass.

Shot Glass

Snowball Shooter

1 part Jack Daniel's®
1 part Rumple Minze®

Shake with ice and strain.

Shot Glass

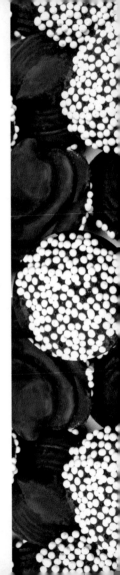

Starburst®

2 parts Strawberry Liqueur
1 part Orange Juice

Shake with ice and strain.

Shot Glass

Starburst® Cocktail

2 parts Light Rum
1 part Pineapple Juice
1 part Sweet Vermouth

Shake with ice and strain.

Cocktail Glass

Sugar Daddy®

2 oz. Gin
2 tsp. Maraschino Liqueur
1 oz. Pineapple Juice
dash Angostura Bitters

Shake with ice and strain.

Cocktail Glass

Swedish Fish® Shot

1 part 100-Proof Blackberry Schnapps
1 part Vodka
1 part Cranberry Juice Cocktail

Shake with ice and strain.

Shot Glass

SweeTart®

1 part Raspberry Liqueur
1 part Sour Mix
1 part Southern Comfort®

Shake with ice and strain.

Shot Glass

Tiramisu Martini

1 oz. Cold Espresso
¾ oz. Coffee-Flavored Vodka
½ oz. Irish Cream Liqueur
½ oz. Spiced Rum
½ oz. Godiva® Chocolate Liqueur

Shake with ice and strain.

Cocktail Glass.

Toasted Almond

1 part Amaretto
1 part Coffee Liqueur
1 part Light Cream

Shake with ice and strain.

Shot Glass

Tootsie Roll®

1 part Coffee Liqueur
1 part Orange Juice

Shake with ice and strain.

Shot Glass

Toxic Jelly Bean

2 parts Jägermeister®
1 part Ouzo
1 part Blackberry Brandy

Shake with ice and strain.

Shot Glass

Tropical Life Saver®

1 part Midori®
1 part Coconut-Flavored Rum
1 part Citrus-Flavored Vodka
1 part Sour Mix
2 parts Pineapple Juice

*Shake with ice and strain. Note: Because this recipe
includes many ingredients, it's easier to make in
volume, about 6 shots.*

Shot Glass

Tutty Fruity Life Saver®

1 part Crème de Banana
1 part Pineapple Juice
1 part Orange Juice

Shake with ice and strain.

Shot Glass

Vanilla Milkshake

1 part Crème de Cacao (Dark)
2 parts Milk
2 parts Vanilla-Flavored Vodka

Shake with ice and strain.

Shot Glass

Twizzler® Twist

1 oz. Cherry Flavored Brandy
1 oz. Anisette
½ oz. Strawberry Liqueur
½ oz. Milk
splash Grenadine

Shake with ice and strain.

Cocktail Glass

Twizzler®

2 oz. Vodka
1 oz. Strawberry Liqueur
splash Grenadine

Shake with ice and strain.

Cocktail Glass

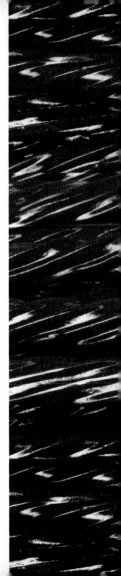

Waffle

1 part Vodka
1 part Butterscotch Schnapps
1 part Orange Juice

Shake with ice and strain.

Shot Glass

Warm Carrot Cake

1 part Butterscotch Schnapps
1 part Cinnamon Schnapps
1 part Irish Cream Liqueur

Shake with ice and strain.

Shot Glass

Wonka

1 part Cherry Flavored Brandy
1 part Amaretto
1 part Sour Mix

Shake with ice and strain.

Shot Glass

Photo Credits

All photographs are ©Gilbert King 2011,
except for the following images ©iStockphoto.com:

Pages 2, 3, 21: assorted wrapped candy; 7: bartending tools; 10: ice; 19: whiskey bottle; 22, 90: vanilla ice cream; 23, 101: red juice; 31: apple pie; 32: green apples; 33, 57, 90: red apples; 34: fish bowl; 37: bananas; 42, 64: cherries; 46, 84: gumballs; 48: black licorice; 49: toffee; 50: candy apple; 53: candy canes; 56: assorted candy; 57: caramel apples; 58: cheesecake; 62, 130: almonds; 64: strawberries; 65: chocolate-covered strawberry; 6, 8 117: raspberries; 67, 69: chocolate flow; 70: cinnamon; 71: oranges; 72: chocolate bar; 73: mint; 73, 97: stick of gum; 78: gingerbread man; 79: gingersnaps; 81: grapes; 81: glass of juice; 82: gumball machine; 88, 132: cocktail umbrella; 100: limes; 101: assorted berries; 109: cantaloupe; 110: peanuts; 110: peanut butter; 114: sandpaper; 116: popsicle sticks; 130: coffee beans; 133: vanilla bean; 136: waffles

Index

143

144

147

Drink Title Index